Once Again ... Love

Reconnecting with the Heart

Sarita Mathur

ISBN: 0620563117

ISBN 13: 9780620563116

To my parents,
Harbans and Sudha,
with love

Table of Contents

V for Victory

The *V* for victory: starting upwards and then plunging deep down to its lowest depths, only to rise up again.

The *V* symbolises the essence of life and love—it symbolises once again-love .Love in itself is always victorious. It is the centre of every emotion, and under all commotion is the absence and need for love.

It is inherent in God's design for us.

God's Design

The universe is round;
All emotions abound.
Some are like Heaven
And some like Hell;
Fear and resentment ring
A bell.
And anger too—
None of these are good
For you.
Under all this, there is
The need for love
In Hell below,
And up to Heaven above:
Seven layers, it is said,
Until you find the treasure
And knowledge which
Will give you pleasure
Buried deep within.
Sparkling demand
Within the heart
But we have to be the
"Part"—the emotion which
Can access it
In the bottomless pit
Of all our fears and desires,
So as to find peace within
And around
Never in doubt
That we can change
The world by changing
Ourselves—

Our heart.
We just have to be the link—
The knowledge of love steadfast.
We
Must not blink.
Yes, we have to be that
Universal truth
Of peace and love,
In the dimensions of Hell,
Earth, and Heaven above.
Love, love, love,
That is the name
Of the earthly game
And God's design
For us.

13th August 2008

I was a Reiki master also, conducting courses in emotional intelligence, for approximately ten years. Moreover, I was a happy wife and mother, living and appreciating the wonderful life I lived.

My answer to the question "How are you?" was always " Great," or "Enjoying life."

In January 2006, we went for a holiday to Egypt then met up with family and friends in Delhi, India. It is always wonderful to be with family and friends in Delhi. Delhi has a pull to it like no other place. Within the chaos of traffic jams lies a wonderful city. The buildings and architecture are worth seeing and its people are varied and vibrant. Nobody can ever get bored in Delhi, and its hospitality in terms of time and food cannot be matched. People go out of their way for complete strangers.

Delhi and Durban are my two favourite cities. Beautiful Durban, with its rolling hills and beautiful beaches, is a tourist delight.

If Kerala is God's own country, Durban is surely Heaven on Earth.

My husband and I went back to weekly walks at the beachfront to enjoy the Indian Ocean.

Shades of blue and green.

Suddenly, I tripped and almost fell, only to pull myself up again.

However, it was not so simple and proved to be life-changing.

Before I knew it, I could barely walk and had to keep resting after every few minutes. The pain was terrible.

Within a few weeks the pain went from bad to worse. It was unbearable—a slipped disc. I was not keen to take painkillers and tried to convince myself that the pain was temporary.

Some years ago in London I had fallen down a flight of steps. I went "aah, aah" and once again "aah," immediately feeling much better.

Healing sounds: this is nature's pharmacy. It is natural healing through sound therapy.

Very few people realize that vowels are healing sounds, and *a, e, i, o, u* help to relieve stress and pain. Babies are natural healers and cry whenever they need anything, be it food, milk, or a change of clothes. Adults too make use of nature's pharmacy, and a good bout of tears makes one feel better.

However, the pain in my back would not
go away.

I was in complete and absolute denial.

How could I, a specialist in energy healing, not be able to cure myself through hands-on healing and meditation and visualization techniques?

Wasn't I in prime health, both emotional and physical? I had a great family life, two young boys, friends, and a passion for life.

This could not be happening to me!

However, destiny has a role to play, and one must face up to the inevitable.

So, after my slipped disc came traction, and when nothing helped, I had to have a back operation.

The operation was a physical success, but my mind was gone—absolutely gone.

The moment I came into consciousness and opened my eyes, I knew that something was wrong—terribly, terribly wrong. I felt suicidal. A chemical imbalance in my brain led to deep depression.

Please help me, I said as soon as I could walk to the reception.

Please tell my parents (they had come from India to help me) and my husband that there is a feeling in my head that I want to die. There is something wrong with me. I need help.

Why Did You Forsake Me, God?

Why did you forsake me?
When you were all I had,
Why did you forsake me
And give me up for dead?
I was so content and serene;
To me, life was just a dream

Achieved and fulfilled.
I was feeling wonderful,
Like a cat that had licked cream.
Why did you forsake me?
My backbone—foundation of life,
Broken and shattered.
Yes, it mattered
That I lost confidence—
I did not want to live
An imbalance in the brain.
I had nothing to give,
Myself or anyone else.
"Wait, wait," he said.
"I am love"—that is true
Both light and dark,
Are part of you.
I showed you the dark night of the soul,
So that you could attain your goal.
You, who knows the Source—
The All that Is;
You, who teach:
I gave you the chance to practice what you preach,
And aren't you happy now?
Curtsey;

Yes, take a bow.
You are peaceful and serene;
The sun shines bright, the grass is green,
And you have achieved creativity—poetry and art.
For you—this is the start
Of wonderful relationships
Between you and me.
Don't you know that I love you?
I have given you the choice of timeless treasure
For your heart's pleasure.
You have overcome the dark night of the soul.
After overcoming the night;
All is bright.
Wonder and happiness still to come,
Morning and noon, until the day is done.
Be happy with who you have become
Beautiful and an admirer of life.
Live, live, live.
You have a lot to give
To yourself and to the Earth.
Creation and creativity is there within you.
Acknowledge yourself—yes, please do.
In the relationship of life and love,
All over Earth and Heaven above.

December 2008

I realised that God is always with you, ready to support you.
When the *V* for victory is at its lowest, it is always waiting to
come back again, plunging downwards to its lowest level and
then peaking again.

One always needs to have faith and get out of the victim mentality. "Why me?" is not the question one must ask. I was reminded of some thoughts I had seen penned down on paper, written by a man who felt forsaken by God.

He saw two pairs of footsteps in the sand: God's and his own. Then he just saw one pair of footsteps and lamented to God that in his time of need, God had forsaken him. He then was told that when he could not walk, God carried him in his arms.

I have written *Once Again—Love* over a few years. In it are penned my deepest emotions and my thoughts and feelings about life.

What indeed is life without strife? Each human being goes through their own personal *V*—the ups and downs of life.

It takes time to overcome these emotions and negativity, but, as *Once Again—Love* demonstrates, life after personal failure is more creative and uplifting, and more fulfilling and joyful, than it has ever been before. It is possible to get rid of depression, anger, resentment, and guilt. Yes, no one can go from depression to bliss without these other emotions taking place. The guilt is terrible, for when you are once again reconnected with your heart, you feel terrible that you created anguish for so many people: generally those members nearest and dearest to you—your heart. However, it is not your fault and never has been. One must forgive oneself and move on. Life takes you on a roller-coaster ride. However, the victim mentality is not good either. You have the ability to bounce back, higher and more fulfilled than ever before.

You can always survive and come back to life's central emotion: love.

Once Again—Love

So many things happen to people,
Events you will never know,
When you see their smiling faces,
Underneath all this show,
There is a reality that they have dealt with,
Which now may seems like a myth.
They have gone through life and love,
Sorted out their personalities and grown
Bigger and more powerful day by day;
In stature, their soul has achieved its goal.
Or tried to,
So that others can also learn and win,
Even within the noise and din. Within earth, our home,
which we must treasure,
It is our heart's pleasure.
In this silent zone,
Where our desire can be met,
We can achieve life's goal
While fulfilling our role,
And Reconnecting with the Heart

13 December 2008

Parents: Mother and Father

When our soul begins its earthly journey, it is brought to Earth through our parents—their genetic code is there for us throughout our life. Genes have an important role to play in life as, of course, our upbringing. Parents are there to love us and nurture us throughout life. However old we may be, our parents will always be those who have brought us into the world, and as such, their love and guidance is a blessing to us.

Parents

From the beginning of time I know you;
You were there for me.
When I first opened my eyes and saw you,
That was the meaning of love for me.
You held me and wiped my tears away,
You shared my laughter with your joy,
And you looked after me night and day.
Whenever I needed strength, I looked for you.
In my weaker moments, I cried by you.
You knew my thoughts, aspirations, and desires.
You know I care for you.
My soul searched for you
And looked night and day.
It wanted to have expression;
It wanted to have its say.
Which parents should it seek
To have a perfect life,
To fulfil its karmic journey,
To live life without strife?
From before time I looked for you;
When I was but a soul searching
For a place on Earth below and Heaven above,
I looked for you;
I didn't rest until I found you
To begin my earthly journey.

Many a time I have told you
How much you mean to me:
How much I cherish and love you.
While you manifest God's glory
On Earth, this beautiful place

Full of people of every race,
From the beginning of time I looked for you—
My spirit had its say.
I am grateful I have you to bless me
Each and every day.
Your love is always there for me to see.
It means the world to me;
Manifesting Heaven on Earth,
My parents are like God in his glory.

God's glory is reflected through our parents. We are destined to be born to the parents we are born to in this earthly life, and destined to the circumstances we find ourselves in.

We chose (as souls) the parents we were born to, so that we can learn and grow in this journey of life.

My Mother

The universe exists because of woman:
The Mother.
Being a mother has helped me to appreciate my own,
Now that I too have grown.
My mother
Taught me to love and appreciate
The human race;
Never to hesitate;
To care and share;
Never a grudge to bear;
And to give worldly goods and love
With the blessings of Heaven above.
My mother taught me to care for the underdogs,
And give them hope:

To educate and co-create their destiny,
To help build homes
And ask for nothing in return.
Not even praise was needed, she said.
Trust in God and yourself.
Work hard and you will achieve your goal,
And in the universe you will play a role
In transforming lives
For humankind.
Give love and do not ask for it in return;
Give hope;
Be positive, and never mope.
And your wonderful energy will spread
And transform lives for humankind.
"It begins with you," she said.
So, this is in appreciation
Of a mother.
I want to be a mother
Just like my own,
My Mother.

Written at Pumula Beach Hotel at the South Coast, this poem is a tribute to my mother. I don't think there could be a person as unselfish as my mother. She believes in economic empowerment and education, and to this end she has contributed enormously. My mother always wants to give more than what she has been asked for. "Give generously, and do not let the right hand know what the left is doing," she says. "You will get blessings when know no one knows and acknowledges your acts of generosity."

Father

A father's place is beautiful,
Something beyond compare;
In the creation of a daughter
A father's dream is there:
In the caring and the nurturing;
In providing food and home;
In giving your child a lifestyle;
And the promises they must uphold.
A father's place is wonderful,
Something beyond compare;
So, Daddy, this is for you,
From a daughter who really cares.

Fathers—they love their children, and their place bringing up a child cannot be underestimated. All human beings have two sides to their personality: the strong and masculine as well as the nurturing feminine. With gender equality and working women, both mothers and fathers share the same aspirations for their children and are equally responsible for their upbringing.

My father played an important role in bringing us up. He retired as a brigadier in the Indian Army. Being a very social person, he loved to party. He is extremely good with children and was always there for us. He inculcated in us a sense of discipline and good family values.

C h a p t e r 3

Soul Travellers

We come into Earth as souls. An innocent baby carries the spark of divinity within its very being. It is intelligent, wise, and innocent.

However, as the innocent baby grows in age, it loses touch with the divine.

We can access this divine spirit within us whenever we want to. When we pray, God listens, and when we meditate, God answers us.

Innocent

I came out of the womb of time
Active and innocent as can be
Yet wise in every way,
Adapting each and every day
In each and every way:
Supreme intelligence at its peak,
Even before I learnt to speak
The human tongue.
I was a spark of light coming
And becoming a part of the world of man
I was really a part of God's plan;
Then as I kept growing and in time became
Wise and intelligent,
It was not the same.
For fear and indecision took prime place,
And in my heart there was no place
For unconditional love.
It is true.
O God! I forgot about you.
But now, realization has dawned on me:
I can still intelligent be
And yet have love and happiness in my heart
When you are a part of me,
Guiding me to fulfil my destiny.

2 December 2008

Soul Mate

Maybe you were meant to be part of my destiny.
And maybe not for a long time,
But only short,
To show me that I needed to learn to be
True to myself.
And you were there to tell my soul
That I was perfect and needed to be compassionate and
wonderful
To me—
Like a soul mate you were there
Just for me to share
Hard times with you and good times too—
But mainly to be comfortable within
My own skin, within my own personality,
And not seek to please
Anybody, anybody at all
But myself — my God.
For in doing that I was
Accomplishing and completing my destiny,
Being part of it in
Compassionate, kindness and joy,
True to myself:
Not an alloy, but pure stillness and tranquillity.
This you did for me, and I cannot do anything
More than thank thee.

Sometimes in life we come across people who have a profound effect on our lives. They might not be in our life for very long, yet even in our brief encounter with them, we know that we are complete within ourselves. These are our soul mates, and they have come into our life for a reason.

Was It a Dream?

Kartik—was it a dream that came to me
When I thought of you beyond eternity?
And you came to me as my son
From another world—spirit
Unfolding into being,
So that you are now all-seeing.
To teach me my goal—
Love and exploration of my soul—
You taught me healing and poetry
In all its beauty.
You taught me fortitude
And how to live life without strife,
With natural health,
Love, and riches—hidden wealth in its glory
Kartik, you taught me to be myself.
And I would love to bless you
And wish you well
In life, present and future.
Find your goals and attain glory.
Kartik, was it a dream that came to me
When I thought of you
And brought you from eternity
As my son, my second one?
Kartik, was it a dream?

An innocent baby, Kartik, was born to us on 21 January 1991.

Through Kartik, Vivek and I learnt about love, life, and, more importantly, how to live life with a laugh and a smile.

Kartik was prone to coughs and colds but developed asthma as soon as we moved to South Africa. He never stopped smiling and laughing, even though he remained very ill. The moment he would be a little better, out would come that sunny smile.

It was because of him that I learnt Reiki (universal life-force energy—hands-on healing that could also be sent at a distance), and that path took me into a wonderful journey of complementary methods of healing. I attended many courses on mind power, alpha mind power, and from feng shui to all the degrees of Reiki and Karuna Reiki (Reiki of compassionate action). I did them all. Souls select their parents, and parents learn from their children just as much as children learn from them.

The Wisdom of the Ages

For Vivek, my husband and soul mate

The old soul said—
In response to
"Why should I go back to Earth again?
Haven't I finished my earthly karma?
Isn't it time to rest
And enjoy life in fulfilment and peace?
I want to be at ease, not enter the world again,
Turning a page for another look in transient time"
(The world—Earth Mother and its biology,

So it is said in mythology,
That Father Heaven and Earth Mother are one)—
The old soul, he said, "Don't you know that someone is
waiting for you—to be partnered to him in life and love,
Which you can't be while in Heaven above? The river
Sarita is flowing around,
Waiting for Vivek consciousness to come around and live
life in harmony,
Like being in a symphony,
An orchestra of beautiful sound,
While peace and happiness abound, and they live together
in harmony."

We are lucky when we have our soul mate as our friend and marital partner.

We are all souls, and when we come into this world, we select the souls we have to interact with in order for us to grow as human beings.

We have to complete the cycle of birth and rebirth, until we are pure enough to once again be part of the divine life-force energy flowing all around us.

Some say that we are entering the angelic realm, while for others it is *moksha* or enlightenment.

Chapter 4

Family

Family
I always feel that if family become like friends
And friends like family, that would be a great thing to be—
The best it can ever be.
For we would be fulfilling our soul story:
Our destiny
To achieve our goal and fulfil our role
In creating harmony and peace,
Always at ease
With ourselves
And our relationships
With each ourselves,
And not bother
With petty squabbles and fights;
For we would live
Life without strife,

Having found peace within
And learned to share,
Knowing that everyone cares
About us,
And having the confidence to be ourselves:
Selfless.

Friends and family are the essence of love, life, and relationships. Both give us the emotional bond that we need to have a healthy and balanced outlook on life. When we live away from our extended families and liken our friends to family, we realize how much our families mean to us.

Quite often we hear people saying that someone reminds them of their aunt, cousin, sibling, or other relative.

Moreover, family members too become like friends; hence, if family members are like friends, and friends are like family, those are the best relationships that can ever be.

Siblings

Born at different times, but from the same womb,
Siblings may be different
And look differently at the same sun and the same moon.
But siblings are always there
To share and care for each other.
Even though far apart in age and geographical location,
Siblings are there for one another in any situation,
Because
They come to Earth as souls
To achieve their goals.
Siblings have a special knack
Of being there

To share
Each other's lives,
Though distance divides them
In physical space.
Yet, they are there to share and care
For each other
And fulfil their pact
Of life and love,
Always to give each other
Comfort and care,
Knowing that the other is there.
Sanjay, I am glad you are my sibling.

Siblings are born from the same womb, and, however far apart they are in terms of physical distance, they will always share a bond that cannot be broken. My brother has always stood by me whenever I needed him. I am even closer to my brother now, and we have even more in common after his marriage to Shalu. My nephew and niece, Gautam and Gayatri, are also very special to me.

My parents, my brother, and I have always enjoyed a special relationship with our extended family of cousins, aunts, and uncles.

My mother always tells me how she was asked at St. Xavier's school (Delhi) as to how many sons she had.

My brother had said that he had twenty brothers and sisters. Of course, he included his cousins.

Both my parents come from big families, and now our family has become even larger and more wonderful, with in-laws from both sides contributing to the diversity of the human experience.

There is always a lot we can learn from each other, once we allow ourselves to do so.

In-laws

In law you belong to me
Just like my own family.
And I know and love you like my own,
For you have shown
Your caring and love to me
By letting me take part in my destiny
And express my individuality in my own way.
In the beginning and at the end of day,
We are connected by law and relationship:
A beautiful string that joy brings
To me and to you.
Like an orchestra, we are different beings living our part;
We are God's gift on Earth,
Our birth
Manifesting in wholeness to bless one another and treasure our growth as souls;
We are together
In law and in love.

I always treasure my in-laws. In India we normally do not tell one another how much we appreciate and love one another. That is taken for granted. Praising someone to their face is to the older generation sometimes embarrassing and almost like you are flattering them or fawning over them.

I feel that if we appreciate good qualities in other people, we must not hesitate to tell them. My in-laws stood by me and had complete faith in me after my back operation.

I was touched by their concern. My husband's *bhua* (father's sister) even came to Durban to be with me when I had depression: low serotonin which suddenly occurred after my back operation.

(Nobody knew the reason—could it have been the anaesthesia or the medication?)

I never told her how much I appreciated her coming, even though she herself may have felt apprehensive about my condition.

Earlier, in India, people did not hesitate to ask, sometimes complete strangers, the most personal questions: "When are you having a baby?" or "Why don't you have another child?"

However, there is also the concept of secrecy: "Don't tell anyone, but such-and-such incident happened."

By the end of it, you do not know how many people have been told. Also, if someone asks you, do you say yes, or pretend you don't know?

However, when I went to India a few months after my back operation, nobody asked me any questions or commented on my condition or lack of it. It took me completely by surprise, as I was nervous about being questioned. Whenever I myself tried to talk about it, everyone just nodded their heads or changed the topic.

I had a very quick recovery from depression (thank you, Margaret Nair) and was absolutely fine when I went to India.

Within a short period of time, I was able to give up all medication—of course with the help and advice of my doctor.

I stopped teaching Reiki (my mother's wonderful advice), as one has to be totally healed and whole within oneself before teaching this wonderful healing modality.

You cannot teach people to be happy unless you are happy yourself. However, my recovery was quick, and once again I started my own healing, complete with feng shui and abstract art. I infused these with the symbols of Reiki for communication and healing. Complementary and alternate healing techniques go hand in hand with allopathic medication, and you do not have to give up one or the other.

I started pursuing my other great loves once again: long nature walks and creating different programmes like Bhangrix.

Bhangrix

After my back operation and chemical imbalance too,
I just did not know what to do;
But waves of creativity swept over me
As I partook of the creative Me.
Painting and craft would my creativity meet,
I would start at 4:00 a.m., until they were complete
Almost every day,
And I devised many programmes too:
One of them was Bhangrix,
A great workout and visualization
For me and for You.
In this I was helped
By Alex
Who was my, and soon our family's, bio-kineticist,
Specializing in the biology and the body's movement:
A rehabilitation expert like no other.

Bhangrix was a one-hour programme,
With toning, exercise, and trance dance too
Chi, Gung, Dervish, Bhangra (Punjabi folk dance)
Trance dance—everything that was good for you.

I also devised programmes and workshops based on The Caterpillar Has Become a Butterfly, based on music and sound healing and emotional intelligence.

I love this phrase with which I named my workshops, and thought I would name my book *The Caterpillar Flew High* with the subtitle *After It Became a Butterfly*, but then opted to go with *Once Again—Love*, and the subtitle *Reconnecting with the Heart*, as I felt that the latter is more appropriate, as I had love that I had lost and reconnected with.

Once again I started reading fiction, realizing that I had just immersed myself in motivational literature, which was needed at that time, so that I could grow and learn while teaching Reiki.

You cannot teach anyone to be strong unless you yourself are strong.

To be an effective channel for Reiki, one needs to heal oneself each and every day.

Sisters

It was not our will but destiny that brought us close:
Sisters , born to share and always to care
For one another.
Sisterhood has always meant to travel any distance of time
and place,
Even though life might become a race.
Sisters are friends.
They are God's gift to man and woman,
And they can and do make life worthwhile.
For, in whatever you do,
Your sister
Can make life worthwhile for you.
And this applies to cousins as well,
For the bond of sisterhood exists beyond the same womb,
So that the nuclear family sustains itself

In emotional well-being with the warmth and comfort of those
Who belong to the extended family of sisterhood.

The bonding of women cannot be underestimated. The sharing and caring, as well as the nurturing and giving of thoughts and emotions, are invaluable parts of life.

Knowing that there is someone out there for you who you can open your heart to or simply just share good times with is an essential component of life.

My life would not be complete without the addition of my soul sister. Not related by blood, Jessie Francis came into my life when I most needed her.

To My Soul Sister, Jessie

A soul sister:
Like no other,
Always to be there,
To comfort and care
And give encouragement too;
Everything will be all right, she would say,
When I would fret
Because of my son,
My younger one,
Who used to be very sick.
Many times we felt that we had almost lost him;
We had a good paediatrician,
It is true, but nothing seemed to work at all.
And the wheezing would continue
All day and all night long.
I then turned to Reiki and alternate therapies—

The beginning of a new life journey—
Whilst always taking Kartik's doctor, Teddy's advice.
Kartik is now big (twenty-two years) and strong,
And in his life's journey, Jessie
Has played a big part
And will always be special to me
And my family
In the continuation of my life's journey,
As a soul, a kindred one who came here to show me
How amazing a soul sister can be.

There are so many people in Durban who have touched my life. Their names are too innumerable to mention.

Nereena, who I used to call my best friend, came and stayed with me whenever Vivek travelled. She came into my life as my Reiki student, and we had good times together. When Vivek travelled, Nereena would come and spend a night or so at my home and was particularly helpful when I was in distress with my back situation. A big source of comfort was she, just like Paramjit (like a brother to me), Kiran, Annamarie, Suchi, and Madhvi. They belong to my family of friends.

Monika and Caro, friends from art
Right from the very start
Of 2003.
Vis was and is like a sister to me and Ponnie and Vis,
With their constant encouragement, help, and advice,
They were there in each and every way
They will remain in our hearts.
For us as a family.
There are many more people to thank and acknowledge:
Wendy Owen too;
She was an invaluable help
And is a friend.

Chapter 5

Peace of Mind

Do we always have to sit and meditate to reach that elusive peace of mind? Or if we just carry on with whatever we are doing in a meditative state, will we find peace?

Elusive

Elusive is that part of mind.
Elusive is that peace of mind;
Elusive is restfulness and tranquillity.
Does God actually show partiality
To those who sit and meditate
With silent mind and the heart in restful state?
Or is it within each human being,
To be thoughtful, all-seeing,
And rejoicing in life as a human being?

On Meditation

You have time to pray
To the Holy Spirit above,
To God and nature,
To rain and the flying dove—
But why is there no time to listen,
To hear with silent mind
The thoughts and reflections
and voice of the divine?
Sit still and meditate;
Reflect upon your own thoughts
And see the manifestation
Of your visualization:
Your dreams answered.
Yes, there is always time.
Listen—and stay quiet.
It is the voice of the divine

16 July 2010

And God Said

I am here and there: everywhere.

Spirit- and God-consciousness are always there for us. All we need to do is listen. When we pray, God listens, and when we contemplate and meditate, God gives us answers through clarity of thought and awareness.

The Present Positive

When positive energy creates positive energy,
Seeping into the soul of ourselves and the divine matrix,
Then we have reached our goal
Of co-creating, with the divine matrix,
Our Mother Earth, and creating perfection within
ourselves,
Evolution being the goal of our spirit—
Our kindred souls, all together in humanity.
Peace—
Just being at ease with ourselves,
Mind, body, and soul,
Co-creating our destiny with the Almighty.

19 September 2008

When we think only positive thoughts and shun all negativity,
then we are in the positive present. We have received the present
(the gift) of positive thoughts, which keep on generating more
and more positivism.

Totality—No Separation

I don't know you in the physical.
But in the spiritual I know you well.
I don't need to know you in the physical
For you in my heart do dwell.
Sometimes I wish you were closer;
You seem so far away.
Spirit doesn't seem close to me.

I wish I had my way.
Yet, when I think again,
I realise I am close to you.
For in my mind's eye, I am with you.
My spiritual eye, it sees you every day.
My third eye, I call it—telepathy at its best,
All-seeing and all-pervading, spirit at its best.

We do not need to see the divine spirit. We have a conscience that constantly advises us as to the right and wrong of our actions as well as our thoughts. Our actions are a product of the energy of our thoughts and emotions.

Once we learn to listen to the divine spirit in our heart, (conscience) we need never feel alone.

Spirit is always there with us, whether we acknowledge it or not.

Solitude

Solitude is not feeling lonely,
As it is not alone-ness.
My solitude is good for me:
To be happy in myself and me,
Knowing that there is no need for anyone's company,
I can enjoy the space I have and need.
I do not constantly have to be active,
For in my soul there is a seed
Signalling spiritual growth.
That is my need,
For physically I possess all that I need for me:
Love and friendship,

So many treasures—I have all my heart's desires
For my mind, body, and soul,
And a healthy outlook
Which comes from spirit,
Not through a book.
It's what life's experiences are about.
To have fun and laughter therapy—
It is exhilarating to participate in laughter therapy,
The ha-ha and he-he,
Of laughter therapy,
Leading ultimately to tranquillity.
Of peace within and around.

Solitude and contentment should go hand in hand. There is never a reason to feel lonely and unloved. If we accept ourselves and love who we are, we can change those aspects of ourselves we are not comfortable with. Once we are comfortable within ourselves, we can be happy with other people.

And God said

I am a specialist, so I think.
For, without a blink,
I can reach
From mountain to beach,
Beyond time and space.
Life is not a race
But an interweaving of relationship and emotions with
thought
And abiding love.
It cannot be bought

But resides within the heart of man-aspects of God,
Source energy at its best:
Love in the heart while the mind is at rest.

We do not have to look for God. Find him—search for him. He is always there within us.

I was born a Hindu and continue to be one. Hinduism to me is a way of life that embraces rightful living and all religions. To be a good Hindu, I do not have to go to a temple, fast, or pray. By living conscientiously and following the right path in terms of behaviour, I qualify as a Hindu. When Hindus pray to the many manifestations of the one divine energy, they are acknowledging God in his many forms. The faith of millions of people resides in the manifestations of the One Source: the divine in the form of the Creator, Preserver, and Destroyer. When we want to pray for knowledge, we pray to the Goddess of Knowledge, who is part of the One Supreme God consciousness.

If we want to pray for the manifestation of a new project, we pray to the God of Manifestation. As human beings, we need something to concentrate our thoughts on, for the divine in abstract form is too difficult to contemplate. There is one God. The faith of a billion people brings powerful energy to symbols and rituals. If you believe that a black cat crossing your path is unlucky, then unlucky it will be. The No 7 is considered to be lucky.

Energy cannot be destroyed. Water heated converts into steam, but when solidified, it is ice. Once it melts, it is once again water.

May 2009

In 2009, Vivek and I went to visit dear friends of ours, Pooja and Vinay Kwatra, in Nepal. It was a wonderful experience. Pooja and Vinay were two of our first friends in South Africa. Their younger son, Amritansh, was born in Durban, and as families we have remained very close. I knew that we would enjoy their company amidst the mountains in Nepal, but did not realize that I would have what I call -a spiritual experience.

Message from the Compassionate One—the Healing Tara
Nepal, 17 February 2009

Peace—that was the feeling and thought that enveloped me when I stood in front of the statue of *The Healing Tara*.

This Goddess of Compassion is the female counterpart of Lord Buddha and has her left hand up in blessing.

I gazed at the statue, thinking of another God, Avalokiteshwar, who I was more familiar with.

Suddenly, I felt myself swaying back and forth as waves of energy washed over me.

The energy waves were so powerful that I had to stop myself from falling down.

It was then that I heard *the voice*:

"Treat everyone on the soul level, and look at intention. That is compassionate kindness."

I took a step backward, and the energy waves stopped.

Was this divine intervention, or a voice from my higher self?

Maybe I will never know the answer, but I am grateful and feel blessed, for this experience has made me aware that I must always think before I judge anyone.

Something easier said than done, but now this thought is no longer an intellectual one.

I must always look at people with heart-based awareness, for on a soul level, we are all connected. Some souls are completely in the light, while others are less so. However, we are all part of the Great Spirit comprising both Heaven and Earth.

The voice of *The Healing Tara* is a reminder to me to always do my best and to remain in the light.

Life is a mystery, but each day of one's life has to be unravelled with love and compassionate kindness.

That is the message of the voice of the Spirit.

With Pooja, we also went to one of the most prominent Shiv temples in Nepal and had *darshan* there. Pooja is a very special person: nonjudgemental and bright. A wonderful poet, she has written amazing prose and poetry on Hinduism, energy, and Buddhist thoughts.

Silver and Golden Spoon— November 2008

Silver spoon in the mouth.
Mine was golden. Yes, I must confess
I was born with both silver and gold.
What did they mean to me?
The Gold ,
It stood for riches—treasures beyond compare:
Love, joy and happiness.
In gold, all was there.

Silver for material possessions:
Abundance in the material world we live in.
Silver for money and riches.
Through hurry and flurry,
Life in a spin.
Gold and silver spoon I had
When I came to Earth.
Material, emotional, and spiritual
Fun, laughter, and mirth.
Both silver and gold are special to me:
Abundance, within and around.
I am happy to be on Earth,
Where prosperity abounds.

While growing up, one heard the saying "she was born with a silver spoon in the mouth." However, I feel that silver and gold must go hand in hand, as spiritual and emotional happiness is necessary for the silver spoon to take effect.

Emotional well-being is necessary for happiness and peace of mind. Money cannot compensate for emotional uncertainty. Both silver and golden are necessary and the gold spoon was imagined by me to be the one for that emotional wellness which leads to happiness .

Why don't we all attract prosperity?

Sometimes people say, "We do not want to be rich."

Similarly, many wealthy people deny their wealth, instead choosing to say, "I cannot afford this" and "If I were rich"

We must be happy with the abundance in our life. When we live in abundance, we can also share abundance.

Sharing abundance creates more abundance. Yes, we need to value both the silver and golden spoons in our lives.

C h a p t e r   6

October 2010
Something Beautiful

Eight years ago, my maid, Dora, passed away. Her sister used to visit her regularly, and after Dora's demise she continued to do so. The seventy-six-year-old would never come empty-handed, but would bring with her fruits and vegetables. I would offer her a meal and money to assist her.

One day, she came to me in distress. She needed Rand 400 and did not have it. She was embarrassed, and she assured me that she would return it as soon as possible.

We moved home after about a year, and I never thought I would see her again. Two years later, she appeared at my door. She had gone to my old house, and the seventy-eight-year-old asked the tenants for my address.

She then asked a security company van to bring her to my place.

Here was Emma with Rand 400 in her hand. "I couldn't come earlier, as I wanted to come with the money," she said.

Not wanting to offend her, I took Rand100 and gave her Rand 300, this time as a gift. Her honesty and determination touched my heart and brought a lump to my throat.

This is the beauty of the human spirit.

So often we judge people because of their appearances or their social status. Honesty and integrity belong to the human spirit and not to a particular age, race, or social status.

M.O.N.E.Y

My Own Natural Energy Yields
A given treasure:
A heart full of pleasure
And delight,
Happiness overflowing from the soul,
And reaching our goal
With thought, belief, and emotion;
Yes, energy in motion,
Emotional intelligence at its best,
Prosperity within and around,
and never a doubt:
M.O.N.E.Y.
My Own Natural Energy Yields,
In material terms,
The soul's treasure,
Thoughts, belief, and action,
The upward motion of energy—emotion
That's what it is all about: MONEY.
My own natural energy yields
Prosperity within

Overflowing in the material world
To give me happiness and pleasure,
Fulfilling my heart's desire.

If you have abundance within you, then abundance will flow outward, and you will also receive in material terms.

Emotional intelligence, happiness, and peace lead to a well-spring of thoughts and actions that attract prosperity to one's life.

You cannot be needy and grasping and attract the physical manifestation of wealth.

Once you realize that you are capable of fulfilling your desires, you will easily achieve them. Abundance creates a vibration of success and fulfilment of desire. It has inherently within it an attitude of gratitude. Think *poverty*, and that is what you will attract; thinking *prosperity* attracts prosperity, emotionally as well as in material terms.

The Nest

The Nest

Birds flying out of the nest,
But the nest remains—intact.
Always having the pact of security and stability
Of warmth and love,
Birds fly upward into the sky,
And time goes by.
They achieve
And in time they build their own,
Their home, their nest—
For they have now found a place to rest,
And are giving life their best.
Children grow and leave their home
But they will always have the security of

Their ancestral nest
And having a rest,
For the nest remains intact.

Arjun

You, who have waited so long
To come to Mother Earth
In its divinity to learn and grow, for evermore
And face the challenge of
Life and love;
You, who have come from Heaven above.
Arjun, amiable and happy
Non- judgemental and bright,
Always trying his best,
To do what is right.
Knowing yourself and spreading
The Light.
Throughout, morning upto night:
A shift and an awakening with compassion and love,
Bringing Earth challenges from Heaven above.
You, who have brought
Change and transformation
And have confirmation of your goal,
I salute you
And am proud
That I gave birth
To one
Who is my firstborn,
My son.

Like birds flying out of their nest and making their own home, children too must find their own wings. They learn and grow, developing their careers and personalities on their way.

Unlike our feathered friends who never come back, children always remain close to their parents whilst attaining their own independence.

Parents must learn to let go. They have done their bit in the development of their child, and now they must be confident that their offspring can make lives of their own. The nest is always there for them to come back to.

Arjun is now a young entrepreneur living in Johannesburg. In South Africa, I came across a new word, *hundreds*, meaning *great*. Arjun is marketing a rehydration drink called 100 Plus and is really passionate about what he does.

May 2011

The Energy of the Eagle

I would do anything for you
So that your life is easier and for you to be
Happy and well-provided for,
But I know that is not to be.
For you have to fulfil your destiny
And know you have the aptitude and skill
To fulfil your will.
You are like an eagle
When it soars high above—
Strong and magnificent in flight;
High up in the sky, observing the wrong and the right;

And *knowing*, as an observer would,
As one door opens, another closes,
And choices are there forevermore.
Life is not a bed of roses,
But an opportunity to learn and grow—
No regrets, just up and go,
Flying up higher, up high
Ever upwards in the sky.
And then downwards to roost and dwell,
As an observer would.
Thoughts and reflections ring a bell
Of the Almighty out there.
Difficulties are there to be,
So that every adversity creates an opportunity
To grow and be, happy in your destiny
By trying to improve it day by day.
Learning and spiritual growth is
What life is all about.
Whether you learn or not, it's true,
You do have an opportunity—
Yes, you do—
To finally be happy
In all you aspire.
As you fulfil your heart's desire
In whatever you do,
My best wishes are always with you,
For you know I love you.

July 2008

This poem was written while both our sons were studying at Durban High School . It is a school with a wonderful tradition of excellence in academics and sport. They believe in the all-around development of each individual learner. Arjun and Kartik value their education at Durban Preparatory High School and DHS.

Like birds flying out of the nest at the right time, your children (also nephews and nieces) have the inherent need to fly out of the nest (home). They have their own destiny to fulfil, and they learn and know the wrong and right of life. Each adversity becomes an opportunity for growth. We must let them move out of the home knowing that we have provided them with love and support, and, as we left our homes to live independently, they too need to go and experience life.

Our love will always be with them, and they have to make their own mistakes and learn from them.

To Gayatri

This young lady who I see;
She is so special to me
And to everyone else,
She is just a teen.
At sweet sixteen,
She is chairperson of the model United Nations,
A cause of great admiration
And celebration of her skills.
She is nice—
a touch of spice.
People around her turn to look,

For she has an inner bright light.
Wonderful and helpful,
That she is.
I saw her as a baby,
And Gayatri is now a young lady,
Doing justice to her name.
She is good at studies and at every game
of volleyball, soccer, and tennis.
Gayatri has many skills;
Family and friends can stand tall;
Because of her personality,
Gayatri is loved by all.

Lots of love to my very special niece
22 Jan 2009

Gayatri is now studying at New York University.

The Owl

The wise old owl
Is more knowledgeable than it may seem,
Looking silently with eyes bright,
Seeing and knowing in the absence of light,
Always protecting mankind
And being an angel, it is true;
For even though people
Are frightened of it,
An owl is a guardian angel,
For me and, of course, for you.
So learn to look
Deep within and see

Let the knowledge seep—
No superficiality,
No double standards.
Universal wisdom is deep,
Personified by the owl,
Nature's beautiful spirit.
It is free.
Never underestimate the owl
On a roof or perched
On a tree.

I have always had a special affinity for this nocturnal bird. I collect owls(in every shape and form)and I soon realized that I am not the only one who has a big collection of owls. My friend, Deepa Khanna collects owls ,be it an owl dustbin, jewellery, painting etc.

I always felt fascinated by owls, and my mother told me that in our family, the owl is considered to be a guardian angel. She said it was the *kul devta* (guardian of the clan).

I want to Be Strong Like the Sun (and like Gautam Buddha)

I want to be like the sun—
The giver of light
To all that is:
To the weak
And the strong;
To the caring
And the uncaring;
To the selfish
And the unselfish;
But
Right now I cannot be
The giver of energy.
For I have to conserve my own
Till I become strong:

My aura rich and pure,
Only compassion radiating from me.
Until then
I must receive as I give—
So that the energy wheel turns
Strongly and silently,
Never depleting me
of my entirety.
And when I receive as I give,
It is like both sides of the coin.
Receiving and giving
Is good for the heart
And good for the soul.
Until I become strong
Like the Buddha,
And only compassion
Radiates from me
Without thought of receiving;
Only of giving
In
a state of serenity.
I want to be strong
Like the sun and
Like the Buddha.

Durban, 2008

This poem deals with thoughts on compassion as well as *giving* and *receiving* .

We all want to be strong like the sun, but until we are, we have to conserve our own energies. When we give without receiving, we become resentful and feel that we are being taken for granted.

Receiving may not be monetary or a gift. Even a thank-you or a smile can be enough to make effort worthwhile.

There are some people who are not takers but very bad receivers.

That, I feel, is not a good personality trait. You have to be a good receiver as well.

When somebody offers you something with love, you must be able to accept it, as it gives joy to the other person. Having a gift rejected is not nice, so both giving abundantly , and receiving with a smile are essential.

I Am Strong Like the Sun

I am strong like the sun
And always happy
When the day is done.
For I have always stood for what is right,
Even when the future was not bright,
And it would be easy to give up and say
Hey, I do not have to have my way.
Let us keep the status quo—
Peace, no need to ask for more.
Yet I am strong like the sun;
It is what I wanted to become—
Tall and straightforward as can be,
Kindness and compassion radiate from me.
Knowing right from wrong,
Yes, I am strong
And can make decisions
And be

Just and fair to everybody,
Including *myself*.
I never forget *me*.
For
I am also a part of everybody:
The Universal Soul,
Happy to be good to everybody.
I can no longer a victim be,
For I am ready to take responsibility.

December 2008

Yes, I am strong, for I have given up the victim mentality and am ready to take responsibility for my emotions and myself. After depression and "poor me" had come a feeling of resentment, which was totally unfounded. It took my cousin, Anu, to remind me that the whole world did not centre on me, and that I had to take stock of myself—a fact that I am grateful for. It takes people who really care about you to tell you where you go wrong.

The Rainbow Nation

After the Party

I saw the rainbow colours:
Violet and green,
Right in front of me
On every TV screen;
Yellow and orange were there.
People all around turned to look and stare
At happy faces;
Bodies dancing;
People talking,
Walking,
And buying *vuvuzelas*
And soccer balls.
Fun was had by one and all,

For it was soccer mania
and soccer fun.
South Africa had the World Cup at its feet.
Clapping and cheering were heard
In every house and street,
Creating once again
A rainbow nation as World Cup rugby had done
All those years ago.
World Cup fever is still here,
People wanting more and more,
And after this party,
A united nation is there
With a legacy to share:
Blacks and whites together in a common brotherhood,
With arms entwined in a common destiny,
With memories to share and care for each other—
A thriving nation, the *rainbow* nation is here,
Not only in the minds
But in the hearts of every South African.
And when hearts are united,
The party will carry on.
Positivity and togetherness,
The effects, will be lifelong;
Yes—this party will carry on.

Reconciliation, Rejoicing, and Ubuntu

"After the Party" was written after the Soccer World Cup, July 2010, held in South Africa.

The excitement was palpable, and, all over the country, flags were flying atop rooftops and on the side mirrors of cars.

Some people had even painted their walls to look like a soccer field.

South Africans of all colour (racial backgrounds) embraced the event and each other. A common sisterhood pervaded the nation.

There was a feeling of *ubuntu* (togetherness; we are one) and of National Pride.

The World Cup brought a nation together to become a *rainbow nation*. The World Cup did what Nelson Mandela did at the time of the World Cup Rugby win: united a nation. It was great for morale-boosting and pride for the nation.

Durban: the Place to Be

Durban. June 2010
I am full of happiness;
I am full of cheer.
It makes me very happy
The World Cup is here.
Everywhere I go I see flags
Fluttering in the breeze,
People smiling and happy,
And everyone at ease.
Proudly South African
And wearing green and yellow,
United are the South Africans:
Child, dame, and fellow.
The Moses Mabhida Stadium
Is an impressive sight to see.
We are at the right place at the right time;
Yes, Durban is the right place to be.

My brother's family came to watch the World Cup in South Africa, and we had an absolutely wonderful time.

Ravi Mama (My Mother's Brother)

Ram, ram, hare, hare,
Hare, hare, rama!
As he walked up and down,
So said Ravi Mama.
After many years of pestering
He came to Durban's shore;
How could we ask for more?
For now we were given the opportunity
To share our hospitality
In our new home
And have him bless us,
As he would;
And we would enjoy and
Imbibe his wisdom,
As we should.
Ravi Mama! What a treat
Just to listen to hear him speak
Words of wisdom:
No platitudes,
Just life,
The wrong and, yes, the right.
Every morning at the start of day,
We would walk on Durban's bay,
And enjoy each beautiful beach:
Umhlanga, Umdloti, and Ballito,
The lagoon and golden mile,
All within our reach.

Vivek and Ravi Mama and I,
Enjoying ourselves galore—
A forty-minute walk, the rising sun—
We couldn't ask for more.
Yet more we had in this beautiful land
Of different languages and races:
Museums and gardens to see,
God's paradise on Earth
Of rolling hills and beautiful beaches.
Yoga, we learnt fr om Ravi Mama,
Kartik, Arjun, and me;
Physically and mentally strong,
That's what life is meant to be.
Ravi Mama came to our home;
After many a month and thirteen years,
As I wrote, I thought it right
To tell him having him with us
Was a real delight.

July 2008

I was so happy when, after years of pleading, Ravi Mama eventually came to visit us.

Having three children of his own (two of my cousins are in America and one in Canada), he is a veteran traveller. However, he squeezed Durban into his itinerary .I asked him to organize a family gathering out here in South Africa and tell everyone what a great country this is and how happy we would be to host them. I have been telling Chitra Mainji (Ramesh Mama's wife), for years to come over, but she too has three children (two in the US and one in Spain), so to find time to come between globe-trotting is difficult.

This year, a big family holiday has been planned in Mexico, and I am hoping that next year, it will be in South Africa.

C h a p t e r   1 0

Once Again—Press Freedom

Like *Animal Farm*, where corruption prevails, even well-meaning socialist governments become power-hungry.

Power corrupts like nothing else. Freedom of the press is essential to keep those in power accountable for their actions, and one must take steps to ensure that democracy prevails. This is possible only with a *free press* to serve *the public's right to know*.

Of course, governments all over the world want to control the press. They are happy when favourable things are written about them and unhappy when reporting is the opposite. "Gag the Press" offers a satire about these governments' desires.

Gag the Press!

The Soccer World Cup (July 2010)
Was a great party, and the press was great,
But now it is terrible and obstinate.

It's time to gag the press
Yes, it's unfortunate when they say
The government isn't stable;
How can they have the cheek
To talk of corruption and nepotism?
It's time to gag the press!
Only when it's favourable,
And the press airs our views,
The media is wonderful; otherwise,
It's time to gag the press!

September 2010

Freedom

In the beginning there was space,
Then the Big Bang:
The word,
Sound, and voice:
The voice of the people.
"For one and all,
Liberation-democracy":
The voice said it all.
Freedom of the people,
The media speaks
Power to the people,
To one and all.
Freedom of expression,
There just cannot be repression.
A single torchbearer of truth

Cannot be extinguished
And can ignite others,
So that there is strength in numbers.
Every government is liberal when it
Comes into power, but—power
Corrupts like no other.
Nobody can stop
The voice of the people,
The voice of the press
Because the economy is in a mess.
And their comrades, like in *Animal Farm*,
Have become slaves,as once again,
Totalitarian rule exists, even though
It is Socialist and Communist rule
And it's government, Communist old-school.
It is against affluence and for workers' rights.
But alas, it has fallen prey to capitalist thought:
Greed and nepotism,
Which can be bought
With money and influence.
These can influence and do.

No transparency out there;
While people starve,
Government does not care.
Muzzle the press, they say,
So that democracy cannot prevail;
Nobody must know what is happening out there;
Journalists must not their views share
And inform people of their
Rights; rulers say, this is blight
On us—our reign.

Muzzle freedom of expression;
For the government, it is a pain.

But one and all should stand up and fight;
The voice of the people,
That is our right.
Press freedom there must be;
It is our land, our country,
And for press freedom, we
Must all stand.

1 September 2010

C h a p t e r   1 1

Rainbow in the Sky

From my bedroom window, I watched the rainbow with awe. To me it was like a miracle in the sky: absolutely beautiful. Immediately I picked up pen and paper, and thus this poem came about.

The colours of the rainbow—*VIBGYOR*, for violet, indigo, blue, green, yellow, orange, and red—correspond to the non-physical energy centres in the body.

From spirituality to communication, intellect to creativity, the rainbow sparks interest in everyone who beholds it. It speaks to everybody. God is indeed there in his glory, asking us to be attracted to light and colour. The world is made up of people of different personality, races, and economic situations. Yet each of them sees the rainbow in the sky, and in effect we have that aspect of divinity within us. God speaks to us in the form of a rainbow.

Rainbow

When I saw the rainbow,
I started to think.
How did it come up so high?
It was like a miracle
In the sky.
After the cleansing effect
Of rain,
All of us were to gain,
Our consciousness
Cleansed,
Even though we were
Drenched.
The rainbow planted a seed
In the cosmic mind.
Light always attracts
The do-er of good deeds.
But wait; I have a
Question to ask
While I in the glory of
The rainbow bask.
Who created this wondrous show?
Is it God taking a bow?
Oh, Creation! We might not know
Who to turn to and where to go.
We might not understand who you are.
Yet we see you in your glory,
You are the sun, the moon, the star bright,
You are the one who
Brings us light.
When the sun goes down;
The moon comes up,

Nature's light in every town.
We just have to see
The rainbow in the sky;
This is not in days gone by
But now up to eternity:
God in his glory.
I see a rainbow
Smiling at me, and I know
You are with me
Always, wherever I be.

The next poem, "Where Will My Spirit Be?" is a nature poem that conveys a desire to be connected to the divinity that resides deep in the soul of every human being. It is an age-old question: Where will we go from here? And further, will we · merge with the divine consciousness? Will we go to Heaven? Will we be reborn again and yet again until we eventually attain enlightenment?

These and more are questions that remain unanswered.

My feeling is that our souls chose to come to Earth as human beings, and, knowing that divinity will always be there for us no matter which sphere we are in, we need to enjoy this experience.

Where Will My Spirit Be?

When I am no longer in this world,
Where will my spirit be:
Up above a mountain high
Or deep within the sea?
Will I be floating on a cloud
Of deep blue, white, or grey?

Will my spirit be sailing along?
Or will it be swept away?

I do not know where I will be,
No matter how hard I try.
Maybe I will just be
A fish or a dolphin,
Perhaps an eagle in the sky.

However, I am happy within.
For I shall be with you.
In your arms you will hold me,
And I will be renewed.

Thank you for all you have done
For me; I thank you again, I say.
I think of you and feel your grace
Each and every newborn day.

December 2008

"Where Will My Spirit Be ?" was a poem which was written by a soul that wanted to escape the world and enter the world of spirit. In metaphysical terms, they say that when the root chakra is touched, the serpent at the base of the spine is disturbed and wants to break free. The spirit soars high, wanting to reach the sky: the world of spirit where divinity is and has been, even though it is unseen.

The root chakra (energy centre) is the centre of tradition, family values, and being grounded.

If the root chakra (base of backbone) is touched by an operation, the spirit wants to break free from the bondage of Earth. It wants to return home and give up the world of physical matter to be one with the divine spirit. This may be a suicidal tendency with the effect of drugs such as anaesthesia or may be just the spirit wanting to break free.

We will never know the answer, but can just speculate
Why certain events happen to people we know,
Who go through life,
The highs and the lows
Only to find
Once Again—Love

Durban Bay at Vacca Matta, Suncoast casino

As I looked in front of me,
All I could do was gaze,
For right in front of me was a body
Of water, in which I saw your face.
I looked at the sky and the ocean below,
And I was filled with happiness,
Though I couldn't understand why.
Waves of contentment swept over me,
And I almost wanted to cry.
All around me I could see
The Universe at its best;
Creative intelligence.
This was it. My mind was at rest.

December 2008

While walking at Durban's Golden Mile, Vivek, Arjun , and I decided to go to Vacca Matta. I asked for a cappuccino (my absolute favourite), and, when the waiter brought it, I requested a piece of paper and a pen. The poem ,Durban Bay at Vacca Matta, was written on a till slip.

The Present Positive

When positive energy creates positive energy,
Seeping into our souls and the divine matrix,
Then we have reached our goal
Of co-creating with the divine matrix,
Our Mother Earth, creating our perfection,
Evolution being the goal of our spirit—
Our kindred souls, together in humanity.
Peace—just being at ease with ourselves,
Mind, body, and soul,
Co-creating our destiny
With the Almighty.

19 September 2008

When we think only positive thoughts, then only positive thoughts emanate from us, creating more positive thought and action. There is no underestimating the energy of the positive thought leading to positive belief and then to action.

We have to learn to watch our thoughts and contemplate as well as meditate on the nature of the universe. There is only one line, one verse, one song: positivism, to which we all belong, and we can find it when we come back to that central emotion, love.

On Meditation

You have time to pray
To the Holy Spirit above,
To God and nature,
To rain and the flying dove.
But why is there no time to listen—
To hear with silent mind
The thoughts and reflections,
The voice of the divine.
Sit still and meditate;
Reflect upon your own thoughts
And see the manifestation
Of your visualization:
Your dreams answered.
Yes, there is always time.
Listen—and stay quiet.
It is the voice of the divine.

16 July 2010

Yes, there is love. Love is in the air we breathe, in the earth, on the ground we walk on, and in the people we see. Even when we can't seem to recognise love and see only its absence in some people and some places, then we know we have to retune ourselves and find, *once again -love,* by *reconnecting with our hearts.*

C h a p t e r 1 2

Women

A Woman Strong

I am who I am:
A woman strong
In body and soul, at peace
And happy all day long.
Knowing I have the inherent ability
To care for myself and family.
I have the ability to be
A seed of divinity:
A human being
Capable of changing the world with
Perfect equanimity.
I can be a lawyer, a chef,
A scientist too.

I can be all that I desire
To make a name for myself and
The human race,
And I have
The grace to be
A woman, a lady,
Perfect within myself,
Raising a family.
It's great to be a woman;
It is great to be.

August 2008

Women all over the world are thought of as strong and powerful. They are nurturers, yet they have the innate strength to be there for their family in any given situation. Women can take up any career and accomplish whatever they set their minds to do. Yet, the world still sees domestic violence against women. Women themselves are unkind to each other and often doubt their own abilities.

Phenomenal Women

Splashes of colour, I can see,
These are the colours of my personality.
Bright and cheerful, with good taste too,
Career woman and mother,
There is nothing I can't do.
Yes, a women is phenomenal
In all she is and can do,
From childbearing and rearing,

From being hardworking to caring,
A woman can be creative.
The world is there to see
A woman is phenomenal;
I am sure you all agree.
So this is to women,
Young and old.
Your spirit is special:
More valued than platinum or gold.
A woman is phenomenal,
That is true;
So, phenomenal woman,
This is for you.

Women in all their many hues and colours are different people with different personalities, each one unique. Women have to be admired for all their achievements.

The People Pleaser

Why do women have the need
Always to please in every deed?

This aim is an obsession, a want,
To sacrifice at any cost.
And it is not the answer,
Said sages old and new:
Relinquish this need and be true to you.
Self is important,
Self-respect too:
In the name of love,
How can anyone shout at you?

Can you not see,
Being true to yourself
Is the reason to be?
When you are honest to yourself
And love yourself true,
You will be frank and honest
And good to others too.
Do not do for others
What they don't ask you to do,
And, by the same token,
Be good to yourself too.
Say no to disrespect.
Put up a fight;
If you don't care for yourself,
Who else will understand your plight?
No one will be there for you
If you don't love yourself true.
Always pleasing others,
Whatever happened to you?
Love yourself first,
And then you will fly high.
Hey, when will this caterpillar
Become a butterfly?

People Pleasers

Always trying to please,
The proverbial daughters, wives,
And mothers, women in general
Sometimes feel resentful
About their roles,
Feeling that living up to others' expectations

Makes them relinquish their own goals.
However, women can be phenomenal;
Women can and do
Choose their own destinies.
Powerful thoughts lead to the energy of action,
And women the world over are catalysts for change.
They can change the world by changing themselves
And their attitudes toward one another.

The visualization below was written for my CD, *The Caterpillar Has Become a Butterfly*. In 1997, I composed a CD on Reiki (universal life-force energy) that has visualizations and a talk on with music in the background, called *Hand in Hand with Reiki*. After this came *Joyful Heart*.

The Caterpillar Has Become a Butterfly (Visualization)

Breathe in and out, slowly letting your body relax.

Relaxing more and more, know that you are in a wonderful state of consciousness: enlightened, knowing and acknowledging the wonderful light within you.

Your light shines forth into the world,

Spreading the energy of love all over the universe.

This light has started within you.

Feel yourself filling up with the twin energies of friendship and love.

Love is who you are and who you will always be.

Love is creation; love is strength.

Love is the ability to set yourself free

And to speak your mind with honesty and clarity.

Unconditional love sets you free—free to be true to yourself.

You are also communicating the energies of truth and happiness to everyone around you.

As you love yourself, the energy of love spreads outward from you. Your spirit is free, and it frees your near and dear ones.

They too can be who they are.

The energy of love is all-pervading, and love commands respect.

With unconditional love and respect for yourself comes love and respect for everyone.

Love yourself, knowing that you have the ability to change. Feel the freedom to be who you want to be.

Deep within yourself, you know you are a wonderful person.

You know that that is true.

Acknowledge yourself, and feel yourself getting a warm embrace from you, your own harshest critic.

You are loved for who you are in this moment of time and ever after.

Be willing to acknowledge this love.

You are free.

The caterpillar has become a butterfly,
And it has set itself and everyone free.

C h a p t e r   1 3

My "Aqua Ladies"

My life is so much richer because of my aqua ladies. Yes, we do aqua exercises in the pool. Multitasking (chatting) we are too, and so the morning aqua class serves as a de-stressor, toner, and an energizer—all at the same time.

Aqua Time

Earlier I used to swim up and down the pool.
The water temperature was cool, and I felt I was having a
great cardio exercise,
When I heard someone speak to me in the next lane.
That was Rosey, who was to become my friend and intro-
duce me to aqua-aerobics,
which occupied two lanes in the morning class at the
Kings Park Virgin Active in Durban,
We used to have coffee afterwards

With Liz, Kathy and Bev;
Cate, Val, and Robin were there too
With Glynis, our instructor, who got into the pool
To exercise with us.
I treasure these friendships so much, and,
All these years at the Kings Park Virgin Active,
I haven't been passive
But have kept fit.
I would never change my gym,
Because it's where beautiful friendships
Were made and kept
And treasured for years.
My aqua ladies are wise and nice,
Always ready to advise on any matter
Of the heart
Or mundane ones as well:
Shopping tips or excursions too,
There is nothing they do not know
Or cannot do.
Yes, they are always there for you.
So, my aqua friends, this one is for you,
For you are part of the sisterhood
That makes life worthwhile,
For whether happy, sad, or life on the mend,
This is definitely a friendship that will never end.

My life is so much richer because of Rosemary Collins and my aqua friends. She introduced me to these wonderful ladies. Liz (beautician), Bev, and Kathy are there almost daily. Honest advice is what friends give when you ask for it and sometimes when you don't. The friendship of these ladies is invaluable to me, and I count myself as fortunate in having these friends in my life. My aqua friends know "everything," and every day is a wonderful day, thanks to these ladies.

Gym

I'm strong and fit and healthy as can be;
As my son Kartik says,
"It's good to have a great body";
A stress reliever it is too,
That's what gym can do for you.
Sociable, it is fun too;
You cannot overestimate the value
Of gym and what it can do for you.

Chapter 14

The Beauty of Friendship

Chakori Gupta

Bird who is in love with the moon,
That is the meaning of *Chakori*,
And the story it tells
Of a lady: a friend,
Practical, nice, and attractive;
Always giving good advice;
A lady of heart and wonderful spirit;
A friend to share your innermost thoughts with.
No judgement there for anyone
But unconditional love.
Chakori, Prads, and Antra,
Living in Mumbai, India's vibrant city
Are people with *heart*,

And I am so glad they're an invaluable part
Of my life's journey.
More like family, they are there,
Always to care
For each of us.
Even whilst they may be busy,
Their lives in a rush,
They belong to our family of friends,
Where friendship never ends.

Chakori and Prads Gupta have been friends of ours since our days in Lagos, Nigeria. We have seen Antra grow up, and they have known Arjun and Kartik since my children were young.

When you live outside your own country, friends take on a different meaning in your life as they share your special occasions and are there for you in times of adversity.

Kathy Ellis

What a friend I have in Kathy—
So beautiful in every way:
Beauty of body, mind, and soul.
She really makes my day.
If I would have my way
I would meet Kathy every day
Or talk to her.
She is an inspiration:
Beautiful beyond comparison,
A friend, mother, and wife
Living life without strife,
And spreading the light.

Beautiful human spirit,
She is fun and really nice,
Energetic, and happy—a touch of spice.
Laughter and happiness is always there.
People around her look and stare
Because of her beautiful glow,
That laughter and smile:
Happy—really divine.
Oh Kathy, you are wonderful:
A friend with one who I can share
Good thoughts and bad ones too,
Always getting a positive from you.
You know you're special
And—I care for you.

Kathy and I met nine years ago. Kartik and John were in grade seven in DPHS, and it was their big farewell, organised by the school and the Seventh Graders' Mothers Committee. That year we had an event organiser (one of the mothers). For the first time, the boys' toilets were also done up in a graveyard scene, and the ladies toilets in a Victorian theme. Kathy laughingly coined the term *toilet tarts*, and this playfulness is part of what made our friendship grow. Pam and Janine were also part of the group, and the toilets were really appreciated. We were told to leave the decorations, so that the whole school would see them the next day.

Sadhna Ramkelawan

Sadhna, my friend, simple and sweet,
With an intelligence and true heart underneath,
I believe in you. You have the personality and depth

To be true to yourself:
A great destiny
Is now yours and still to be,
As you achieve your potential,
Your beauty unfolding more and more
As you grow each minute of each day.
If I had my way
A queen of hearts you would be,
Teaching by your example
Of love and care.
Beautiful Sadhna,
It is true:
I believe in you.

I first met Sadhna Ramkelawan when she came to attend my Reiki courses.

She carried on to become a Reiki master teacher. All through, her sincerity and dedication impressed me. She is really a wonderful person. We became good friends and continue to be so.

These three people I have written about are with whom I have what I call low-maintenance relationships.

We may meet once in a blue moon—sometimes months will pass before hearing from each other, but whenever we pick up the phone or have the opportunity to catch up with one another, there are no recriminations—no saying "Why didn't you call?" or "Where are you?" Kathy and I often greet each other by saying "Hello, stranger."

It's lovely having such good friends, and I could not resist adding this chapter to my book, because of course it is about love, life, and relationships.

When I was in school, I used to write poems on my friends, and after 2006 I started to do this again. These friends have been with me in my change, growth, and transformation and are essential to the story of *Once Again—Love*.

C h a p t e r   1 5

School Calls—Once Again MGD

Maharani Gayatri Devi:
My alma mater
In Jaipur's Pink City
Is the manifestation of a dream come true
For Rajmata Gayatri Devi,
A boarding school for girls and day-scholars too;
This school is wonderful and has a very good tradition
Of excellence, and the school motto, "Our utmost for the highest," will be with me throughout my life.

The school song, "Oh Come, Let's sing of MGD," tells us to "think of the happy hours. Think of the carefree days."

The blessings of MGD are there with every girl who had the good fortune to study there.

Yes, they were happy days and continue to be so.
MGD'ians all over the world are united
In the blessings of their alma mater.

There is a sisterhood that exists because of school, and we are all reaching the manifestation of the dreams we had while at MGD.

I went for the Diamond Jubilee celebrations of my school and reconnected with many of my school-mates. It was a wonderful feeling.

Three years ago (2009), I once again went to visit my friend Madhulika (Mishra) Naithani, and together we went to MGD.

There was a real feeling of nostalgia while we stood in front of the school building and took photographs.

We were taken on a conducted tour, and we revisited our childhood.

Madhulika was a day scholar, and her mother was my local guardian in school.

Over some weekends, she would come to fetch me from school and then to drop me back once the weekend was over.

I was really touched that this family went out of their way for me, even though my parents did not know them.

During the holidays when I went to Delhi, Nandita Sardana Kochar would come by bus to pick me up from my grandparents' home to take me to Ashok Vihar, where she lived.

She would come by bus to drop me back again, as I was not sure of the way. I am still in touch with her, and we remain good friends. Mukta too is in Delhi, and it is important to me to keep up with old friends.

Anjleen and Sharmila (both boarders and dear friends) are probably the first to know before I reach India for our annual holiday, and I have visited Chui (Sujata Morjaria) in Kenya.

There are so many others—good friends to keep in touch with.

I also joined Facebook when I realised I could get in touch with old friends. Earlier I felt that I would rather contact everyone personally over e-mail or phone, but when Chui said that it was a great way of keeping in touch with MGD graduates, I immediately joined the social network.

Chapter 16

Building Bridges and Playing Cards

It all started with my husband, Vivek, wanting to learn how to play bridge.

I hate card games and find them extremely boring, except for the three-card game, which we play for fun during Diwali (the festival of lights). That is really a social game and great fun.

However, when my friend Vis enrolled for bridge lessons, I got the number from her, and Vivek and I learnt bridge with Jan Chemaly.

Jan took us into a new phase of life with her bridge lessons .She is an excellent teacher and always there for you whenever you have queries. Vivek and I , now partner each other, leading to a new and exciting phase of life, almost (but not quite) becoming bridge addicts. We felt we knew a lot of people, but were surprised at how many more we came to know and care about. Bridge really does activate the left brain (logic and numerical activity) and is highly recommended not only for the middle-aged and elderly but also younger players.

The bridge community is very caring, and so many people, including Jeff and Heather, have become part of our bridge family.

Bridge Is a Game of Life

Bridge is a game of life,
Though it is a card game.
In life, you are dealt
Many cards;
In retrospect, they are the same.
The ace and the two,
Each one is good for you.
The ace might look strong
And victorious,
But never underestimate
The humble two,
For in adversity it might
Be good for you.

Life is a game of cards,
And you have to play it well
It is the bridge between
Happiness and depression
And each life has a lesson to tell.
Life and Bridge teach us
To always do one's best
Whatever cards we are dealt with—
Our knowledge put to the test.
Trust your instincts;

It is in the play.
But follow the conventions
In bridge, and lead a principled life as well,
And then you will see the rest.
Give the game and life your best.
Bridge is a way of living:
Treat everyone the same;
However, distance yourself from the losers,
The unhappy ones who
Make you moan and fret,
And concentrate on life's play.
God has brought you
To this Earth to learn the divine way.
Two people have the same life,
But how they deal with it will differ always,
So just learn to be happy and
Enjoy bridge—life's game.

March 2009

Bridge of Life

Two years later and with a better understanding of it

Bridge is a game of cards as it is of life,
With happiness and strife,
Acceptance and caring,
Never despairing of your partner's ability
To communicate and navigate
The pitfalls and bumps

The no-cards, which are bound to come
In life as in cards;
However, it always changes,
And if you defend well, you will succeed
And make life a pleasure,
As it is indeed a treasure.

So live life without strife,
No pouting and no shouting,
Childish behaviour, or bullying
Your partner or others,
In bridge as in life.
Be understanding, for with every failure
Comes new understanding
And new ways of dealing with life
And the hands you are dealt.
Accept with gratitude the ace
And the humble deuce.

East, west, north, and south,
The winds of change come about.
So abide by the rules;
The conventions are clues
And tools for good behaviour.
Life is full of smiles if you want it to be—
Partnerships and friendships
Made and kept forever.
For bridge is meant to be good for the brain:
An addiction that is positive,
Also known as brain food.
Even though sometimes people
Get off track and break the rules,

Being good at bridge should make us
Understanding and kind,
Leaving all impatience behind,
As we all make mistakes,
Even though we have a stake
In the outcome of the game.
Building bridges and playing bridge
Are key to a better life.

Happiness—no strife
Of caring and sharing,
Improving the quality of life.

Two years later, bridge is still an important part of our lives, but now a new term has come into our dictionary: the *bridge divorce*. Bridge friends now have to take one or the other person's point of view, and sometimes it becomes difficult for them, just as in life.

The bridge divorce is sometimes necessary yet painful. There is the same feeling of regret and of being let down by one partner or the other. Rejection also has to be dealt with, and as in life, there are feelings of insecurity.

There are often recriminations from both sides. However, life goes on, and as in life, sometimes the bridge divorce does not end the feeling of friendship and camaraderie.

One has to live by conventions in bridge just like in life; you have to live by principles and good behaviour. Playing bridge together and having a good partnership also makes you closer to each other. The bridge community in Durban is a very strong community. The warmth and friendship of people is there to see, and complete strangers go out of their way to help others out.

Avondale Club in Clarence Road, Durban, is a particularly nice club. Helpful and caring, they give you tips on how to improve your game. (It has now amalgamated with Durban Duplicate and continues to be nice.)

You see the best of people when you play bridge, and of course you see the worst.

Another important part of playing bridge is "losing the ego."

People are not happy to lose and feel disgruntled when they do not do well.

Many people learn to play bridge when they are older and have achieved some standing in life. Hence, they are not happy when they make mistakes and sometimes cannot take the competitive feeling in duplicate bridge. The trend is now changing as younger people take to this wonderful card game of strategy.

I play socially as well, and my Tuesday afternoon is my bridge afternoon with Jill, Penny, and Meg—a wonderful way to spend the afternoon.

Chapter 17

Nigeria—Once Again

This name may bring a shudder;
When you think of the country, however,
You are wrong and advised to think correctly, for
It is a nation with a lot of warmth
And hospitality;
Women
Are respected, and
Children loved and cherished.
There might be crime and criminals there
But they do not shoot
To kill.
If you give what you have
They will let you go unhurt.
The men with flowing agbadas,
The women bright and free,
Having broad smiles and happy looks

In this populous West African country.
There is a bad element there,
But definitely not the whole country.

We lived in Nigeria from 1986 up to 1995. They were happy times, and both our children were born in Lagos. We did not have a single instance of crime. My husband learnt Pidgin English and till now enjoys speaking it.

Arts and crafts in Lagos are worth looking at, and their beadwork is really special. It is home to authors of great repute, including Chinua Achebe and Wole Soyinka. I had the good fortune to meet Ken Saro Wiva at the book club, where we read books by African and Caribbean authors. I met Karen King Aribisala there as well, and she still remains a good friend and continues writing excellent literature.

Lagos is home to a large Indian expatriate population. There are many Lebanese out there, as well as Europeans, Canadians, and Americans. Many of them belong to the oil companies Mobil and Shell, and of course the diplomatic community has a strong presence..

We will always cherish the friendships made and kept in Lagos. These friendships will remain with us throughout our lives. I learnt to value my Indian education, as I could hold my own in any conversation and book review. Whilst in India I had always felt that Europeans and Americans don't care about their children and are always happy to see them leave home. However, I realized that this was a misconception. I also learnt to embrace the Nigerian people, knowing them as warmhearted and full of humour and hospitality. When family is not there, then friends play that role, always to bring comfort and care. My maid, Chemenzi, played a very important role in our lives, and everyone who knew us in Nigeria remembers her. The

parties in Lagos were legendary, and one had to learn to cook
and share.

Your culinary skills played a big part, in Lagos times.

Lagos Times

The wonderful parties out there:
Beach outings on Tarquay Beach,
Shopping at Lekki Beach,
Ikoyi, and Victoria Island;
Yes,
Vivek and I were there;
I learnt silk painting,
Aerobics as well,
And to appreciate African art
And the people out there.
When it rained,
And the water clogged the streets,
Electricity was gone for days to come;
The men and women smiled and laughed,
With their children in their arms
And small babies tied on their backs.
I also saw a video
Of Shaka Zulu,
And was excited to know that we were now
Going to another part of Africa:
South Africa,
Our home would be.
I remember Patrick (our chauffeur), who wrote to us,
after we left for South Africa, "After you have left, I am no
longer Patrick."
We were touched by his affection,

Though strong and aloof he did seem
While we were out there,
Except to our son, Kartik,
Who he loved,
As Kartik was born
While Patrick worked for us,
We trusted him completely;
Also Amazing Amezi
(Office worker was he).
So many memories of Nigeria
Are coming back to me;
Maybe after eighteen years a visit is due,
I have been told that in Nigeria there are many changes to
see
And I will definitely go back to this populous country;
Once again—Ikoyi Club, a place to meet
Going to Falomo
And buying caftans on the street.
Once again, Nigeria
Beckons to me.

$$C\ h\ a\ p\ t\ e\ r\quad 1\ 8$$

Two Restaurants on Florida Road

Florida Road
Cubana Lounge vs. Spiga D'Oro

I walked into Cubana Lounge on Florida Road
Happy and cheerful, not at all bored,
For my son's birthday: a surprise, it was meant to be.
Why don't I make a booking for him and us three?

There is no booking available—there is no escaping the fact.
It is packed to the brim with people, thin and fat.

However, Luke said,
Come on April the third on the eve;
Have a drink or two—you won't have to leave.
(The place is big.)
Wait till other diners finish their meals.

Cubana Lounge is great—it is a real steal.
So on the third, my husband and I came to eat at Cubana and
enjoy the same.
My husband (well dressed and handsome too) looked the part,
as I did too.
Two bouncers at the door: "You cannot pass!
Do you have a booking?" they asked.

I called Luke—he was off duty, he had said.
"However, take my number, as no landline yet."
Do you remember me, Luke?
Just two days ago—
You said I must come, although no booking I had.
Yes, he said—I cannot understand.
"Are you not dressed well?" he asked.
"Yes, I am, and my husband too."
"Can you speak to them, and see what you can do?"
The hostess said.
"Well, I don't know"—maybe the gentleman was not wearing
proper shoes.
High-fashioned sandals he had on:
A statement to his good taste and mine.
The manager was called, and the hostess our case explained.
Luke told us to come, we said.
"I can't do anything," he had said from afar,
Not bothering to ask what our statement or cause was.
The hostess shrugged, What can I do!
"Do you want to speak to the other manager? Do you?"

No, no, I said, that is all right—but do you see,
Inside and to your right,
Shorts and sandals are there to see—

No dress code, as far as you can see?
Lots of empty chairs are there too:
Place for us and others too.
Sandals and shorts——did you see!
Yes, she said, "What can I say——
Let me call the other manager."
No, no, I said, "Let this one have his way."

Onward we went,
My husband and me, to Spiga Doro,
Where we felt free——free to be.

No hypocrisy there, we could see.
So drinks we had and dinner too.
The waiter and the manager welcomed us too.
So pleasant they were——Jason and
All the three——
So Spiga Doro is the place to be:
Just like Cubana lounge, a place to dine.
The attitudes so different.
It is Spiga every time.

Oh, Spiga D'Oro
With plate, mug, and bowl.
You have captured the warm spirit
Of the African soul. Keep up the spirit.
One person can make a difference.
You are all we need for the rainbow nation.

So, from near and far, we can rejoice.
We all have the power of choice.
Cubana Lounge, with bouncers there to see,

Do not forget—you represent the hospitality industry.
And Spiga D'oro,
with plate, mug, and bowl,
You have captured the spirit
Of the African soul.

These are two restaurants in Durban's Florida Road; Cubana Lounge and Spiga D'Oro.

Cubana Lounge was burnt down a few years ago, but now has risen from the ashes. We have not been back again so cannot really say whether the controversial attitude still remains.

However, Spiga has become our favourite restaurant. It is vibey, and the food is excellent. I love payment cafés. After the Soccer World Cup, Spiga has expanded and is a full-fledged restaurant.

After my experience, I wrote this poem and sent it out to friends. I did not expect the immense response as it went from one person's mailbox to another. People forwarded this poem, and others e-mailed Reply to All, and soon quite a few people were sharing their experiences at these two restaurants. One person wrote saying that she could not believe how someone got chucked out of a restaurant and was foolish enough to write a poem on it. Interesting—I had said what I wanted to and did not reply to any comments.

LIPS (Live Poets Society)

L.I.P.S. pouting, smiling, sternly commanding
L.I.P.S. – cheerful, happy
Sometimes irritable
Sometimes snappy
But always having a story,
A human one
Straight from the heart
For all poets are a part of the human fraternity
From now up to eternity
Poets have a story to tell ,of life,
Happiness and strife,
And the Live Poets Society
At the Point Yacht Club,
(it has now moved to The Collective)
Enjoying the ocean and the city's hub
Is a wonderful mix of people

All of them have warm hearts
Embracing life…
Welcoming people into their midst
As they did me.
I must appreciate how much knowing them has added to
my life
Thank you, Danny,
Because of you I learnt about LIPS (the Live Poets
Society)
And I appreciate your warmth;
And Hannah, a special thanks for your
encouragement—always.
LIPS, individualistic and true—I love being amongst all of
you.

12 July 2010

I love going to my monthly meetings at the Live Poets Society. There is always a guest speaker (poet), and after a brief interval, it is an open-house session, where all attendees can read out their poetry.

I was invited to be their guest speaker in 2010, which thus enabled me to compile all my poetry. Though I had it on computer, it was scattered in different places. From then on I started writing excerpts to it, and *Once Again—Love: Reconnecting with the Heart* was born. I have had the privilege of listening to many different poets of all ages, races, and economic backgrounds, all speaking and sometimes enacting their creativity—straight from the heart.

BOOK Club

I am also part of a book club (Durban chapter of the International Book Club).

When a friend, Avinash Hiranandani, asked me if I was interested in joining a book club that his wife, Mansha, and he were starting, I jumped at the opportunity. Being part of a book club by Indian expats has exposed me to diverse and wonderful people. We have read a variety of books from all genres. Every month, there is a book review, and the person whose chance it is to give the book review selects the book.

Chapter 20

The Age of Technology

The age of technology—for all its information and knowledge at one's fingertips, the age of technology is actually making us strangers to each other. Family members are no longer giving one another undivided attention, while friends are talking to other friends, even when they are together. We are in the cocoon generation, where the thumbs keeps clicking and typing, and there are constant beeping messages interrupting our conversations.

I turned when I heard someone say hello.
Who could it be, I thought as I had come for a walk all alone,
Only to realise he was talking on his cell phone.
I know that the world has become smaller
Through the coming of the Internet age,
Facebook, and Twitter;

They have become the rage.
Communicating electronically with everybody,
We have become strangers to ourselves,
With no time to talk to family.
What about the folks at home?
We need to learn communication
To achieve manifestation of our goal.
In life,
Our soul has a role to play.
Too much technology creates imbalance;
Our emotional self will have to pay.
Progress in the material world
Should be linked to our spiritual self.
These are just my thoughts;
It is time to reflect.

Mankind

Is man really kind?
And are human beings really being true to themselves?
Or are they busy doing—doing,
Just not happy with being;
True to themselves,
Something, just anything
To stop their minds from being still,
Always ready to pop that pill.
Something to sleep or to stay awake,
Creating a drama to wallow in.

Rather than being calm—at peace,
Where the mind is at ease
And positive thoughts reign.

C h a p t e r   2 1

The Mole and the Whistle-Blower

At the end of every night, there is day—light always prospers.

The mole and the whistle -blower are ever-present in most large corporations, governments, and even in religious institutions.

Every human being has the power of choice—and brave and honest people have always stood up for their beliefs, facing great odds and unpopularity.

What is the point of going to church, mosque, and temple unless we practice what we learn in these religious institutions, the pillars of moral society?

And do these religious institutions always guide us to fair and just behaviour—to stand up for our own rights and let others have the freedom of choice to practice what they believe is right?

Standing up for what is right and having the courage to take action is what the whistle-blower is all about. For every mole burrowing deep within and demolishing society, there will definitely be a whistle-blower.

The Mole

5 October 2008

A mole came out of the dark—out of the black night.
Uncertain and unsure, he came out into the light.
A company called; "Come out for a future bright,
Where you will have a say,
Food, security, honour, plus abundance and good pay."

The mole, startled, ran back and forth;
Is this the end of dark?
Then it ran to grow and prosper
In a company set-up.

It worked, ate, and drank,
With all the other folk;
Slowly, he corrupted them.
They were honest before.
Bribes, and sweet flattery.
The mole was full of talk,
It was efficient as well;
It corrupted the entire staff.
The acted against their employers;
They sold their souls.
Personal enrichment and dishonesty,
That became their goal.
"We are together," the mole said.
"I am up to the task;

Work silently for me,
You will in glory bask.
Riches, I will give you.
Trips—to and fro.
Double income you will have,
As *me and you* continue to grow.
The mole found out their weaknesses;
He had a hidden plan:
He kept the employees within his grasp.
They were afraid to be taken to task.
Their lies and weaknesses ,he exposed;
Their families, he told.

As they agreed to his dictates,
He grew more and more bold.
The mole came out of the dark,
Rubbing his hands in glee.
He would not depart
Until he dragged, one by one,
Each employee;
His deed had to be done—
But, alas for him, a giveaway,
A whistle-blower—for him it spelt the end of day,
And night it was to come.
As two employees saw the light,
And threw off his clutches,
Though they remained in fright,
Scared of his might.
Eventually cornered, the mole gave up,
Confused that his game was up.
"What happened?" he thought,
"When I had everyone bought

With sweet seduction, money, and gift,
Who then told on me and committed a rift,
Even after I played the race card?
They showed me that might,
collusion, and dishonesty was not right,
And would not be tolerated.
For the mole, the end was in sight—
Once again, darkness,
For him the end of light
But for the others, another chance.
Bring in the light, let us dance
In light; shun the dark.

As teenagers, we face peer pressure and are taught to stand up for what and who we believe in.

It means saying no to drugs and avoiding doing or saying anything that is against our value systems.

As adults, we face the same choices. Sometimes these choices are difficult for us, and we have to suffer the consequences of our actions.

The Mole Part 2

After the mole left on its own,
Afraid of its plight,
Knowing that the end was in sight,
The company smiled in glee,
Much before its time.
For another mole was there to be,
Burrowing deep within,
Eroding the company, and to see
That nothing new was uncovered;

In the set-up, he played a part,
Thinking that this was the start—
He was now king!
For he had played his part
In keeping quiet and pocketing within,
While giving the honest ones
Hard work and claiming spirituality,
So that there was partiality towards him;
Another one had to bite the dust, and another one went,
but not him
For he had been bribed by the Original One.
In the company there was a riot,
The transporter went to and fro,
Material reaching through the door,
To his home while he did roam,
Pretending to be at work.
Eventually, though, his game was up
And he did on everyone tell
And wanted them punished as well.
In fact, he tried to insist,
"If I go down, then everyone else must as well;
I may not be the mastermind.
There is another one of my kind."
The company then cleaned up its act and made a pact
For transformation and change to come.
The end for most and relief for some.
Good always prospers and in the end;
There is always light at the end of night.

The mole is dangerous, for he corrupts everyone within
sight. Like a bad apple contaminating all the rest, the mole corrupts all who come into contact with him. That is why one must

always be careful of the company one keeps. Sometimes, the people who put up an honest front and seem to be impeccable in behaviour and character are the ones you must watch out for.

The Mole, Part 3

The company groaned and shifted to and fro;
When will all this end?
We are driven around the bend;
So many people have left
Or have been asked to go,
Now we cannot ask for more
But be happy with the status quo—
However, in came another one who had changed his ways
From the very old days,
Long ago, when he did work in the company set-up,
Before his time was up.
"Give me another chance," he said,
"Let old times be laid to rest;
I will be good for you and efficient as well;
We must not on the past dwell."

The company forgot about his past,
But alas, it was the start
Of corruption,
But of another kind.
For now a control freak was in sight,
Sulks and indiscipline he did bring
And tantrums throw,
Efficient at work and moody within.
Everyone was frightened; this was an attack from within.

The control freak
Walked to and fro,
Messing with the office folk;
Fights and backbiting started to brew;
This was something new.
Also, there was another story;
It really was the crowning glory,
For he had a partner in crime,
Ready to take his side every time.
Who could it be? A traitor in the enemy house?
Well—no one other than his spouse.
Eventually, though, all was well,
And the company rallied around
With a smaller staff;
Professionalism and honesty,
This was really the start—
Beginning of light,
And end of dark.

December 2008

Forgiveness is important, but the question must be asked: Why did the person change his ways? Did he go through rehabilitation or have a spiritual/religious change, or has he got a mentor? Otherwise, old habits die hard, and the mole continues to carry on as before.

The Inverted V

The inverted *V* starts from the top and goes down on both sides. We are at the pinnacle of successful growth, but moods and emotions are part of every human being. However, we can always come back to that height of heartfelt awareness and contentment.

Reaching God

1 February 2009

Even when I was diagnosed with clinical depression, I always knew that I just had to find God Consciousness once again.

I prayed for it and asked for help, for I knew in my heart that I had to reconnect with it. My spirit—my soul needed to be healed. I had been teaching spiritually guided life-force energy for ten years. This had helped a lot of people. With Reiki, you are a channel for the life force and can take no credit for this wonderful healing energy.

> O God, let me reach,
> In thought and speech,
> Higher and more noble,
> My thoughts igniting
> Words of wisdom and compassion,
> Love, laughter, and passion for life.
> Let me feel the vertical force
> From Heaven above in the sky,
> Coming down to Earth—
> The horizontal force,
> So that they meet
> At the centre
> And spread to one and all:
> Offices, homes, markets, and stalls,
> Peace above and underneath,
> Where Heaven and Earth meet.

When you ask, you will always receive. I had support from family and friends. Though I still do not know and understand how a simple back operation left a happy, content person with a chemical imbalance in the brain, I gave up being a victim. I had good doctors looking after me as I went from hospital to hospital.

My friend, Vis, gave me good advice in the early days. Herself a medical doctor, she told me to take stock of myself and to "stop being a victim."

God

If I get up in the middle of the night
And call your name,
Will you think of me
As I do you?
Will you
Turn in your sleep,
Take a leap in consciousness
To be close in thought
(Feelings that cannot be bought)
And reclaim me as your friend—once again?
This is what we were till I transgressed,
But I still feel it wasn't me;
It was my mind:
Morning to night
Voice in my head,
Until I went to bed,
And still remembered
You—
Oh God, I never forgot about you.
Please take me back as your friend;,
Yes, please do,
So that I can rise up again
In thought,
Sunshine, or rain,
Until I find love—once again,
And reconnect with my heart.

Yes, I always knew that I would find the connection, but it would take time. My husband and two sons were amazing at this time. I felt terrible knowing how my state of mind affected them and what a lot they had to deal with.

I was really blessed. Arjun was in his twelfth year in school,
but he never blamed me.

"It's not your fault, Mom—don't feel guilty."

Vivek and Kartik were equally so, as were all our friends
in Durban. They were and still are like family to me. Added to
this were family and friends overseas who were supportive with
phone calls and knowledge. If one has to go through mishaps to
find out the meaning of love and friendship, then I am lucky to
have had this experience.

Even If

The night is dark and forbidding,
And fear looms in the heart,
Lightning in the sky, and storms in the sea,
The creative Spirit is there in you and in me.
God, the Divine One, is there,
Even though waves thrash about,
Heralding tsunamis and earthquakes;
The oceans break; and men and women in fright
Scream and shake;
Even then there is hope,
Reconnecting with the heart, and rebuilding of Mother
Earth;
She is not damaged beyond repair
By the actions of man.
Drugs are an addiction and now there is
An additional form of addiction:
The medicinal one.
So many people popping pills:
Sleeping pills
Without prescription

And tranquilizers too.
None of these could possibly be good for you—
I too have been an addict,
Sucked into a dark dangerous world
By a combination
Of anaesthetics and drugs,
Struggling to break free—
Or could it just have been my destiny, as said by my
astrologer
(Colonel Dhankar), that I was destined to
Have a back operation
And medicines and anaesthetic and drugs are part of the
process.
I had this feeling after I woke up that insects were crawl-
ing all over my skin,
Voices in my head, telling me to do intolerable things,
All to me.
Cravings for food—an insatiable appetite.
However, I always knew that there would be an end of this
night;
Hope to me was always in sight as I asked for help;
I had family and friends,
Good doctors too;
They brought me to the mend;
My broken soul was healed and whole.
I will not wish this on anybody,
But yes, I do know,
That I survived and came out strong;
Creativity just spilt out of me in the form of poetry
and art
As I reclaimed the poetess in me.
In art and craft I was always interested,

Books had been my passion too,
However, after this upheaval—this storm—
I found the divinity within me.
I became logical too;
My left brain was activated,
And I became a different personality.
Yes, I needed this to happen to me as I partook of my
destiny.
It took time and from low serotonin (a chemical imbal-
ance in the brain)
And a process of depression, anger, and pain;
None of this was in vain
As I learnt to manifest my will
In seeking God's way.
After a period of frustration and guilt,
How could I be this way?
Anger and resentfulness had never been my way.
I lived to grow strong each and every day.
Before I was a victim,
Of *poor me* and *how did this happen to me*;
But now I was strong:
Strong like the Sun.
This is what I had wanted to become.
I am enjoying God's grace,
Living in the rainbow nation,
South Africa—nation beyond comparison.
Durban—piece of Heaven on Earth,
Beautiful ocean and rolling hills.
The grass is green—not on the other side, but here within
And around us,
For we can achieve perfection,
By changing ourselves,

Our heart;
So, if the goal is to end corruption and crime,
Root out anger and jealousy too,
We just have to change one heart, starting with our
own——
Our hearts
So that we can change the world by changing ourselves,
Becoming the change we want to see,
As said Mahatma Gandhi,
Not judging others, but always doing what is right,
If another one falters, we must still be upright
In all we do;
With behaviour and emotions,
Be still and access quietude.
Within that priceless gem that is within us:
Our heart.
Our conscience , we must always listen to,
Whether in noise or peaceful solitude.
As it will always tell us what to do.
For when we are in that silent space,
We will always be within Heaven's Gate.

I came out of this terrifying experience in my life strong and confident. However, it took me almost a full year to completely give up on prescription pills (which were necessary at that time; I even had to go in for ECT). The main problem for me was accepting that this helpless person could possibly be me. After a year, I once again went back to doing Reiki for myself and took the help of all the alternate therapies I used to teach. This spiritually guided life-force energy sustains me, and I am very happy that I was a student of Colonel Mann, who is a dedicated and compassionate Reiki master.

Never

Did I a cigarette smoke;
Alcohol never suited me,
I knew I do not have to imbibe spirit to enjoy life,
For I have the spirit within me.
Happy and joyful it often is,
Sometimes sorrowful too,
Yet I was always sure I could connect
To the divinity within me.
So I wrote this book
In poetic prose, so that whoever reads can know,
In a very creative way,
That love is the centre of all emotion,
The absence of which causes commotion,
And all you have to do is be still:
Contemplate and look deep within
To find the seed of divinity.

I learnt to be non-judgemental about people, and now, whenever I hear of a brain attack, I listen first before writing anyone off as mad or crazy, for sometimes there are situations beyond your control that happen to you. You cannot go from deep depression to bliss straight away, but have to go through anger, resentment, frustration, and guilt to find

Once Again—Love.

So many things happen to people,
Events you will never know;
When you see their smiling faces
Underneath all this show,
There is a reality that they have dealt with,
Which now may seem like a myth.
They have gone through life and love,
Sorted out their personalities, and grown
Bigger and more powerful day by day;
In stature, their soul has achieved its goal
Or tried to—
So that others can also learn and win,
Even within the noise and din
Within Earth, our home, which we must treasure,
It is our heart's pleasure
In this silent zone,
Where our desire can be met;
We can achieve life's goal
While fulfilling our role
And Reconnecting with the Heart.